Norman
INVADERS
AND SETTLERS

Tony D. Triggs

Wayland

Invaders and Settlers

Norman Invaders and Settlers

Roman Invaders and Settlers

Saxon Invaders and Settlers

Viking Invaders and Settlers

Series Editor: James Kerr

Designer: Loraine Hayes

Consultant: Mark Gardiner BA FSA MIFA Deputy Director, Field Archaeology Unit (Institute of Archaeology, London).

This edition published in 1994 by Wayland (Publishers) Limited

First published in 1992 by Wayland (Publishers) Limited, 61 Western Road, Hove, East Sussex, BN3 1JD

British Library Cataloguing in Publication Data
Triggs, Tony D.
   Norman Invaders and Settlers.—
(Invaders & Settlers Series)
I. Title   II. Series
942.02

HARDBACK ISBN 0-7502-0620-9

PAPERBACK ISBN 0-7502-1354-X

Typeset by Dorchester Typesetting Group Limited
Printed and bound in Italy by Rotolito Lombarda S.p.A., Milan

Cover pictures:
Top left: Norman lettering.
Top middle: The ruins of a priory.
Top right: Norman-style clothing.
Bottom left: A Norman castle.
Bottom middle: A picture from a Norman book.
Bottom right: Route of the Normans to Britain.
Back: *Domesday Book*.

Pictures opposite:
Top: Norman lettering.
Middle: Some wealthy Normans.
Bottom: A Norman castle.

CONTENTS

All words that appear in **bold** are
explained in the glossary on page 30.

The Normans arrive

The Normans lived in Normandy (part of northern France) but in AD 1066 a large Norman army led by William, Duke of Normandy, sailed to England. They defeated the English in the Battle of Hastings.

The Normans knew that the English were good at many things. They were skilful farmers who made woollen cloth from their sheep's wool. They were also excellent sailors and traders, and the Normans bought shiploads of English cloth. However, the English were bad at fighting on horseback. The picture below shows how they fought on foot while the Normans charged at them on their horses. The English tried to defend themselves by making a sort of wall with their shields but the Norman horsemen knocked them down and trampled on them.

William became King of England. Because he conquered England he is known as William the Conqueror. William and the Normans ruled strictly and the English had to obey them. Some of the women in southern England were good at **embroidery**. The Normans forced these women to use their needles and brightly-coloured threads to make a set of pictures called the Bayeux Tapestry.

This picture from the Bayeux Tapestry shows some English soldiers on a hill-top and some Normans riding up to attack them.

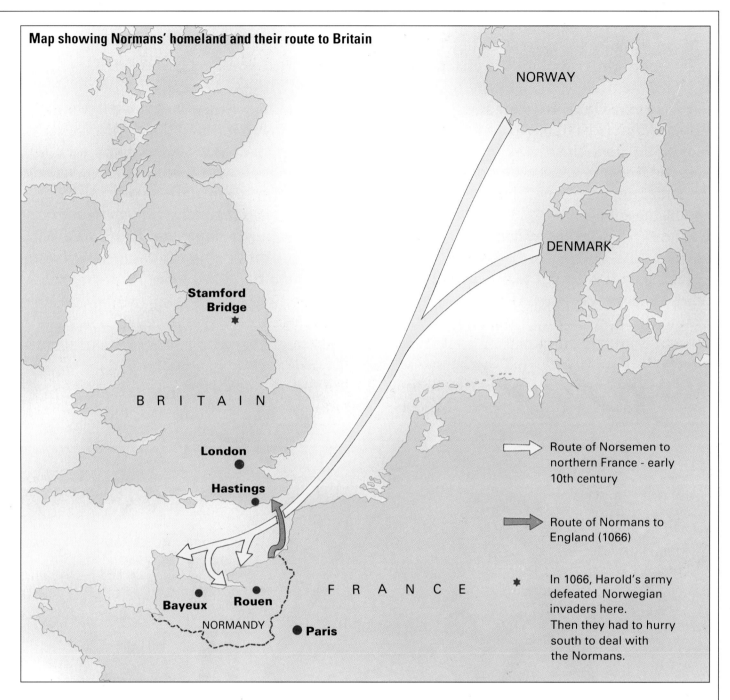

Map showing Normans' homeland and their route to Britain

NORWAY

DENMARK

Stamford Bridge

BRITAIN

London

Hastings

Bayeux   Rouen

NORMANDY

Paris

FRANCE

⇨ Route of Norsemen to northern France - early 10th century

⇨ Route of Normans to England (1066)

✱ In 1066, Harold's army defeated Norwegian invaders here. Then they had to hurry south to deal with the Normans.

The Tapestry tells us the Normans' reasons for conquering England and it also tells us about the Battle of Hastings. The women sewed the pictures on strips of cloth, and joined them together to make a very long strip. When it was finished some Normans took it to Normandy. They hung it up in Bayeux Cathedral and it went nearly all the way round the walls. Most Norman people could not read, but the Tapestry was like a comic strip; it was very easy to understand, and it made the Normans feel proud of themselves.

The Tapestry starts with a picture of Edward the Confessor, who was King of England from AD 1042 to 1066. Edward is sending a man called Harold on a friendly visit to Normandy. Other pictures tell us Harold got on well with Duke William.

We even see Harold making a very solemn promise to serve and obey Duke William for the rest of his life. Then Edward dies and we see Harold taking over as king. Duke William believed that Edward and Harold had promised to let *him* be the next king; he felt that Harold had cheated him and broken his word. The next pictures show Duke William preparing some ships to carry his army to England. The Tapestry ends with the battle itself – and William's victory.

People had different ideas about what William was like. According to a Norman **monk**:

William was the wisest, most generous ruler in the world…He was fearless in danger…He spoke well and was good at getting people to agree with him.

An English monk did not like William nearly so much. He said William was:

…stern with people who tried to go against his wishes. No one dared to upset him because he could be so violent. He had rich men put in chains for disobeying his orders…People who lived under William had a very hard time and they suffered a lot.

Harold died in the Battle of Hastings, but we do not know how. In this part of the Tapestry, someone seems to have an arrow in his eye. In the next part of the Tapestry, someone is being struck with a sword. Either could be Harold – or both; perhaps he was killed with a sword after being hit by an arrow.

Domesday Book

William kept parts of England for himself. He let the churches have other parts and he shared out the rest among his richest followers. These wealthy men, called barons, built castles to keep themselves safe from attacks. (The barons were afraid of the English and they were also afraid of each other.)

Each baron let his Norman friends build houses in the villages throughout his lands. There was usually just one Norman family in every village. The man was called the lord (or man in charge) of the manor. A manor included the lord's house and land, and the neighbouring village.

In AD 1086 William decided to find out as much as he could about England. He wanted to know about its villages, farms and other things like mines and forests. He wanted to know who owned each patch of land, what was on it and what it was worth.

According to an English monk: *William's men went to every county and found out its size and what land and cattle William owned there, or how much the people ought to pay him in* **tax** *every year.*

They also found out how much land his followers owned, and how much everyone else possessed in land or cattle. He had it done so carefully that they noted every patch of land, however small, and every ox, cow or pig. (It is sad to have to write about this but he did not seem to mind doing it.) All the records were taken to William when they were ready.

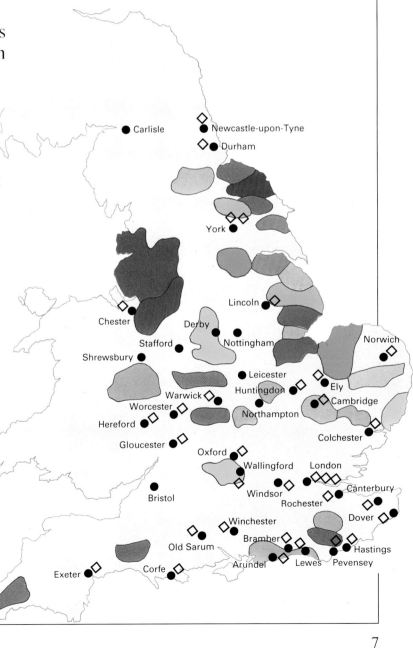

Estates granted by William I to Norman barons

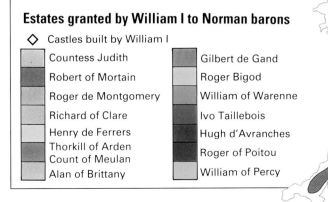

◇ Castles built by William I

Countess Judith	Gilbert de Gand
Robert of Mortain	Roger Bigod
Roger de Montgomery	William of Warenne
Richard of Clare	Ivo Taillebois
Henry de Ferrers	Hugh d'Avranches
Thorkill of Arden Count of Meulan	Roger of Poitou
Alan of Brittany	William of Percy

The monk makes it clear that the English disliked what William was doing. They feared that he would increase their taxes or take their property and give it to Normans. Some of the English tried to tell lies about the amount of land or cattle they owned, but William was ready! He sent a new team of men to each county to check the facts and catch the cheats.

The monk was wrong when he said that William's men did not miss anything out. Even so, the King finished up with more information than he required, so he had the main things copied out into booklets. There was one for each county, and soon after William's death in AD 1087 they were made into two huge books which are known as *Domesday Book*. 'Domesday' means day of doom or judgement. The name shows that people thought the work was very important. It helped the kings who followed William to run the country, and today we can use it to find out what England was like at the time. Here are some of the things it says about a place called Ashby in Leicestershire:

*In Ashby, Edgar used to have enough land for five ploughs pulled by five teams of oxen. Now Drogo has two ploughs there, and two Frenchmen and a fighting man share the rest of the land…There is a **vineyard** and there are 60 **acres** of woodland where pigs can get acorns and other food.*

One of the volumes of Domesday Book.

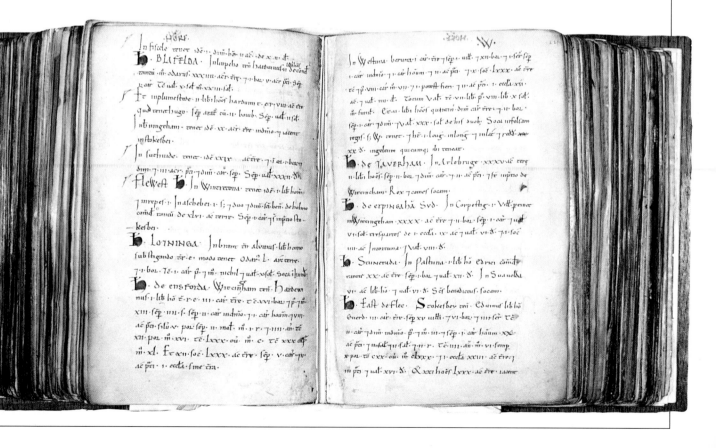

Making a frieze

A frieze is a long strip of pictures or decorations made to go round a wall. The Bayeux Tapestry is a frieze that tells a story. Perhaps you and your friends could tell the story of *Domesday Book* in a coloured frieze. It could go round your classroom wall.

Use your imagination to make a list of scenes. One scene could show some cheats being punished; another, at the end, could show a king looking at *Domesday Book* and receiving taxes. Share the work out carefully before you begin.

You could include some beautiful lettering on your frieze.

Studying the Bayeux Tapestry.

Castles

The Normans probably made the English build castles and houses for them. They even made English men fight in their wars.

Many Norman castles were built on hill-tops. This gave the soldiers a good view of what was happening all around; they could see any enemy troops before they got too close. A castle on a hill top was also very hard to attack; enemy soldiers had to scramble up the hill while the men in the castle shot at them with arrows and hurled things at them.

ABOVE *The Norman castle at Chepstow in Wales.*

BELOW *The Norman castle at Ludlow in Shropshire.*

The Mote of Urr in Galloway, Scotland. The large oval ditch protected the bailey; the small round ditch protected the motte (the mound for the wooden keep).

The first Norman castles were very simple. A wooden fence was built round a few wooden buildings at the top of a hill. Then the Normans built a ring of stone buildings instead. The outer walls of the buildings did not have windows, and this made the ring extremely strong.

The Normans also built castles with huge square **keeps**. A tower at each corner made the keep stronger and gave the soldiers an excellent view. Beside or around the keep was an area known as the bailey. The bailey had buildings where soldiers lived. It also had places for blacksmiths, **brewers** and other workers. There were stables for horses, and yards where cattle were kept until they were killed and eaten.

Some Norman castles were built in towns. The castles were huge, and in Norwich and Lincoln many people had to pull down their houses to make enough room. Once they were finished, the size of the castles frightened the English, and so did stories of people being punished and killed in the gloomy **dungeons**.

For extra safety, a castle had a deep ditch round it. The Normans sometimes filled the ditch with water and turned it into a **moat**. The moat had a bridge which the Normans could raise to keep enemies out.

Life in a castle

The keep was the strongest part of the castle, and the baron lived there with his family, servants and other staff. These included a **priest** to say prayers, and **scribes** to write **documents**. The family's main room was called the great hall. It filled the middle part of the keep, though the walls were so thick that a chapel and other small rooms could be fitted into them.

Inside the keep of a Norman castle – a scene from a film. The film-maker has had to use his or her imagination. Read the next page and decide whether you would make the castle look this clean.

Defending a castle

The barons could only go hunting in peacetime. If another baron attacked the castle, a baron's family and soldiers had to shut themselves and their animals inside the keep. The attackers might surround the keep for weeks or months, hoping that once the people had eaten their animals, biscuits and other dry food, they would starve or give in.

Water was very important indeed, and every castle had a well in the keep. The attackers hoped that the well would run dry, and they looked for ways to poison the water. They also hoped that **plague** and other diseases would spread in the filthy, overcrowded conditions. The defenders fired arrows from the windows and roof. They did not give in easily because they were afraid that their enemies would torture and kill them.

The attackers sometimes tried to break down the walls of the keep, or its massive door. One way to do this was to hurl rocks across the moat from enormous **catapults**. Sometimes the attackers filled in part of the moat with soil and stones. Then they ran at the door or the walls with a tree trunk called a battering ram. When the attackers got too close to the walls, the men in the keep threw rocks and boiling oil on their heads. The bravest attackers tried to climb the walls with the help of ladders or special towers on wheels, but they rarely survived. A safer way of attacking was to tunnel under the walls to make them crack and fall. Even this had its dangers; sometimes the tunnel collapsed and crushed the men to death.

Pleasures and pastimes

Hunting was a pleasure and also a way of getting food. In addition, it gave Norman barons and knights a chance to practise riding and **archery**. This was important, since these were skills they would need in war. Large parts of England were covered in forest, and the Norman kings took most of the forests for themselves and their barons. They stopped the English hunting there, and some of the poorer people went hungry. Others carried on hunting in secret, but if they were caught, they were punished very severely. Some were killed, some were imprisoned and others had their hands cut off.

A film-maker's view of a scene from a jousting tournament.

Out hunting with a hawk and hounds. Where do you think this picture comes from?

Quintain jousting.

Jousting, like hunting, was a way for rich Normans to have a good time and also get themselves ready for war. In a jousting contest, a pair of horsemen rode at each other with **lances**, trying to knock each other out of their saddles.

Poorer people invented a form of jousting known as quintain jousting. Instead of aiming their poles at each other, the horsemen aimed their poles at a board or a wooden figure. It was safer than proper jousting but it was still rather risky. Look at the picture above and try to decide what could happen to horsemen who hit the figure. English villagers gathered to watch and laugh as their friends and neighbours took part.

There was plenty of outdoor entertainment. Jugglers, acrobats and people with performing bears went from village to village. Young people also took part in all sorts of sports and games, including jumping, wrestling, swimming and skating. In winter they played chess, backgammon and other board games.

Many English women had to make their families' clothes. Spinning and weaving wool to make cloth was very hard work, but once the clothes were finished, women often embroidered patterns on them. They also did embroidery on spare bits of cloth. Norman women could afford to buy fine linen cloth from English **merchants**. They preferred it to the woollen cloth worn by English people because it felt more comfortable next to their delicate skin. But like the English they embroidered some of their clothes to make them look more attractive.

Men, women and children all liked dancing and singing, and poor people sometimes made simple flutes from sticks or bones. Many Norman families had proper instruments. These included early forms of the flutes, horns, violins and guitars which we still use today. They also had drums, and the drummer tapped out the rhythm while other people played, sang or danced.

Women's clothing from Norman times was like this.

The Church and the monasteries

Some people thought that too much pleasure turned people's minds away from God. They became monks and nuns and they spent their lives in separate **monasteries**, where they prayed, worked extremely hard and obeyed strict rules. At meal times they had to listen while someone read them the rules or part of the Bible.

A bishop (a very important priest) speaking in the open air.

The ruins of a priory (a sort of monastery) at Castle Acre in Norfolk.

This house in Lincoln belonged to a merchant. It is one of the oldest houses in Britain. To have lasted so long, it must have been finer and stronger than other Norman houses.

Some monks and nuns had to work with their hands; others had to teach, study or copy out books. They were not allowed to have any property of their own; being poor was one of the most important things in their lives. However, churches and monasteries became very powerful and very rich. People gave churches and monasteries gifts because they thought that this would increase their chances of going to heaven when they died. People always took a gift for the church when they went on pilgrimages (journeys to pray in holy places).

Some towns (like Walsingham in Norfolk) grew up round holy places. There were inns and shops for visitors, and monasteries for those who wanted to live and pray there for the rest of their lives. Monasteries needed workers, and their houses helped to make the towns larger.

Other towns grew up where people from villages came to trade with each other at markets. Some towns still have markets today, and many began in Norman times.

It also gave them light and helped them to cook their porridge or stew. Sometimes it also destroyed their home!

Women did housework and cared for the children. The following passage gives an idea of how hard a woman's life could be:

…a stray cow is lapping up all the milk. The clay pot is boiling over and her husband has come in grumbling.

Rich women could own land and have other people working for them, but life for poor folk in villages was very hard.

Most villages had a church and a priest. The priest did not have to grow his own food; the villagers gave him a share of their crops. The priest and the lord of the manor both had barns for storing what the villagers gave them.

The lord of the manor usually lived in a large stone house with quite a lot of land all around it. Other homes had tiny gardens for growing vegetables, but the villagers grew most of their crops in fields. There were usually three fields in every village, and each villager farmed some strips of land in every field. Each person had strips in different parts of each field, so good bits of land and bad bits of land were shared out equally.

One field was used to grow wheat or barley, one was used for peas or beans and the other was used to graze sheep or cattle. Every year the villagers changed the way they used each field:

peas and beans

cows and sheep   wheat and barley

The animals' dung helped to keep the land healthy and good for crops, so the villagers made sure that every field received its share!

25

Draw your own map

The pictures on this and the previous pages help to show what villages were like in Norman times, but each village was different. *Domesday Book* shows that Boughton in Kent was very small:
The lord of the manor had one plough; and there were three villeins and two cottars with one plough between them. There is a church, some meadow, and woodland for sixteen pigs.

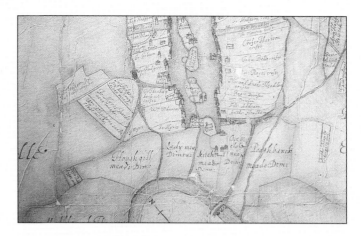

Draw a map of a similar village, deciding the layout for yourself.

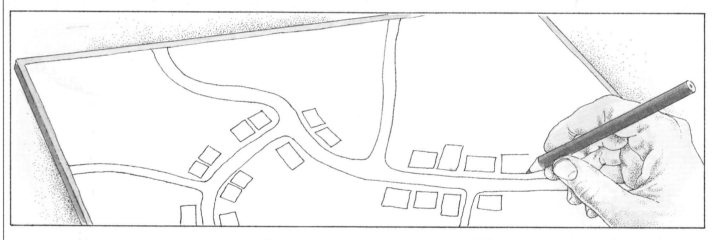

Draw boxes like this ☐ to stand for the villeins' and cottars' homes.

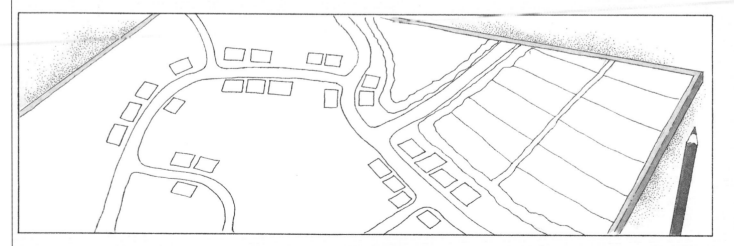

Draw dark lines to show the hedges round fields; draw faint lines to divide the fields into strips.

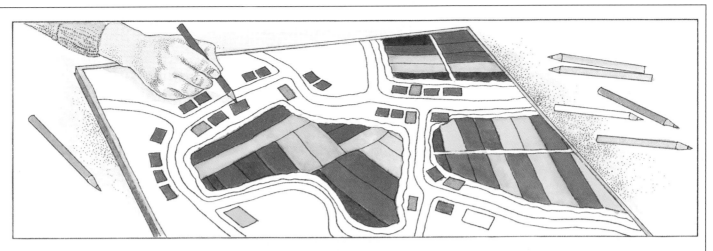

Use three colours – one for the lord's home, one for the villeins' and one for the cottars'. Use the same colours to show which strips of land they farmed. (Give the lord of the manor the biggest share.)

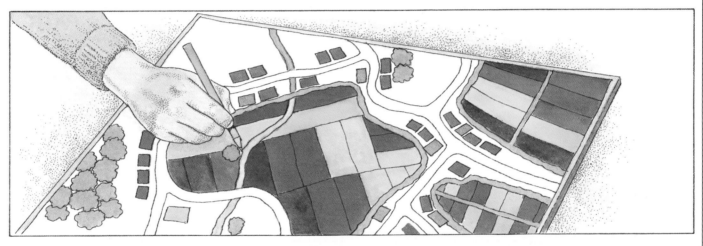

Add other things that the village might have had, but don't make it too complicated.

If you are good at drawing you could turn your map into a picture like the one on pages 24-5.

After William the Conqueror

Three Norman kings ruled England and Wales after William the Conqueror. The first was William's elder son, who was also called William. The second was William's younger son Henry. Finally, William's grandson Stephen came to the throne.

None of these Norman kings conquered Scotland. Scotland had kings of its own, and a Scottish princess married William's son Henry. She and her youngest brother David went to live in England. Then, when David became King of Scotland, he returned there with some important Normans. They built castles and started to make the poorer Scots obey them.

Stephen died in AD 1154. There were no more Norman kings or queens, but Normans living in England and Wales did not seem to mind. This was partly because many of them had married English people. Their children were half Norman and half English, and they usually thought of themselves as English. The first Norman settlers in England spoke a form of French, but by AD 1154 almost everybody spoke English, except in special places like law courts.

Many French words were added to the English language. This came about in various ways. For example, the Normans

This stone font (a bowl for baptising babies) in Winchester Cathedral was carved when England was ruled by the Normans.

This page from a Norman book shows the four Norman kings. The artist has tried to say that they were holy men who believed in God. How has he done this?

learned the English names for farm animals but they stuck to the Norman words for the animals when they were eating them! When cow was served they called it beef, when sheep was served they called it mutton and when pig was served they called it pork. Soon the English began using these words too.

The Normans also brought new ideas about law and government. *Domesday Book* is an example of the careful way they ruled. This care still affects the way things are done. For example, the Norman-French words *'la reine le veult'* (the queen desires it) appear on some official documents.

We can see other signs of the Normans all round us. Some of their larger buildings survive, and so do some of their customs and games. Norman boys and girls taught their English friends to play conkers, and children in Britain still play conkers every year.

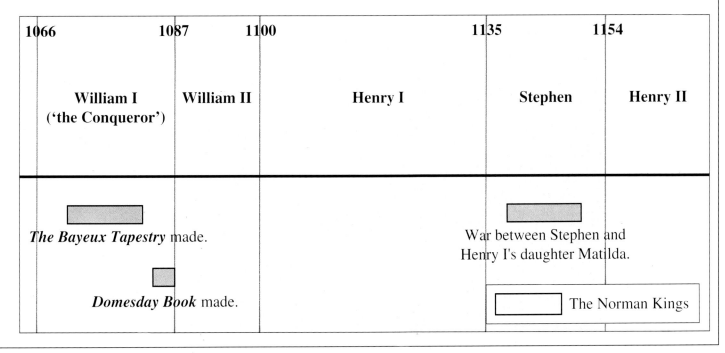

1066	1087	1100		1135	1154
William I ('the Conqueror')	William II	Henry I		Stephen	Henry II

The Bayeux Tapestry made.

Domesday Book made.

War between Stephen and Henry I's daughter Matilda.

The Norman Kings

Glossary

Acre A unit used to measure land. One acre is roughly the amount of land in a medium-sized field.

Archaeologist Someone who studies remains of the past.

Archery Using a bow and arrows.

Brewer Someone whose job is to make beer.

Catapults Weapons for firing rocks.

Documents Important things written down to be kept.

Dungeon The cellar of a castle.

Embroidery Making attractive patterns and designs with brightly-coloured threads.

Graze Eat grass.

Keep The main building of a Norman castle.

Lance A wooden pole used as a weapon.

Merchants People who earn money by selling goods.

Moat A water-filled ditch that defends a building.

Monastery A place where people go to live and worship God.

Monk A man who lives in a monastery.

Plague A dangerous disease which used to be very common in Britain.

Priest A minister of religion.

Scribes People whose job is to write things out.

Tax Money which people have to pay to the king or the government.

Thatch To cover a roof with straw.

Thresh To beat stalks in order to get the seeds.

Vineyard A place where grapes are grown for making wine.

Books to read

The Castle in Medieval England by J Burke (Batsford, 1978)

Domesday Heritage by E Hallam (Arrow, 1986)

A Guide to Norman Sites in Britain by N and M Kerr (Granada, 1984)

Living Under the Normans by D Cameron (Oliver & Boyd, 1978)

Norman Britain by T D Triggs (Wayland, 1990)

Norman England by P Lane (Batsford, 1980)

The Normans by J Nichol (Blackwell, 1980)

The Normans by P Rooke (Macdonald, 1981)

Places to visit

Bamburgh, Northumberland: castle
Boothby Pagnell, Lincolnshire:
    manor house
Buildwas, Shropshire: remains of
    monastery
Bungay, Suffolk: castle
Canterbury, Kent: cathedral and
    Eastbridge hospital
Castle Acre, Norfolk: castle, priory and
    town remains
Castle Rising, Norfolk: castle and church
Dalmeny, Lothian: church
Dunfermline, Fife: church
Durham: castle and cathedral
Ely, Cambridgeshire: cathedral
Fountains, North Yorkshire: remains of
    monastery
Heath, Shropshire: deserted village
    and chapel
Inverurie, Grampian: castle
Leuchars, Fife: church

Lincoln: cathedral and houses
London: British Museum, Museum of
    London, Tower of London, Victoria
    and Albert Museum
Lumphanan, Grampian: castle site
Much Wenlock, Shropshire: castle site
Norwich, Norfolk: castle, cathedral and
    'Music House', King Street
Old Sarum, Wiltshire: castle and
    cathedral site
Pembroke, Dyfed: castle
Reading, Berkshire: the museum
    sometimes has a copy of the Bayeux
    Tapestry on display.
Rievaulx, North Yorkshire: remains of
    monastery
St Davids, Dyfed: cathedral
Southampton, Hampshire: houses,
    town wall
Tyninghame, Lothian: church

Index

The numbers that appear in **bold** refer to captions.

Picture Acknowledgments

The publishers would like to thank the following for the pictures used in this book: Lesley and Roy Adkins 11 (top); Aerofilms 12; Ancient Art and Architecture Collection 19 (top), 21, 23; E T Archive 29; Michael Holford 4, 6, 18 (bottom), 20 (bottom); Kobal 13, 18 (top); Topham 9 (bottom), 10-11, 26 (top), 28; Wayland Picture Library 8, 9 (top), 14, 15 (top), 19 (bottom), 20 (top), 22 (bottom); Tim Woodcock 22 (top).

Artwork: Peter Bull 5, 7, 15 (bottom), 26-7; Peter Dennis 16-17, 24-5; Malcolm S Walker cover (bottom right).